American CULTURE & CONFLICT

Living Through THE VIETNAM WAR

Clara MacCarald

Rourke
Educational Media

rourkeeducationalmedia.com

Before & After Reading Activities

Before Reading:

Building Academic Vocabulary and Background Knowledge

Before reading a book, it is important to tap into what your child or students already know about the topic. This will help them develop their vocabulary, increase their reading comprehension, and make connections across the curriculum.

1. Look at the cover of the book. What will this book be about?
2. What do you already know about the topic?
3. Let's study the Table of Contents. What will you learn about in the book's chapters?
4. What would you like to learn about this topic? Do you think you might learn about it from this book? Why or why not?
5. Use a reading journal to write about your knowledge of this topic. Record what you already know about the topic and what you hope to learn about the topic.
6. Read the book.
7. In your reading journal, record what you learned about the topic and your response to the book.
8. After reading the book complete the activities below.

Content Area Vocabulary

Read the list. What do these words mean?

administration

ally

assassinated

draft

guerrillas

journalists

lottery

Pentagon

veterans

volunteers

After Reading:

Comprehension and Extension Activity

After reading the book, work on the following questions with your child or students in order to check their level of reading comprehension and content mastery.

1. Why did the United States enter the Vietnam War? (Summarize)
2. Why is the Vietnam War considered part of the Cold War? (Infer)
3. What did the Gulf of Tonkin Resolution do? (Asking Questions)
4. Name a country where U.S. troops are fighting today. Do you know why they are there? (Text to Self Connection)
5. Why did the Soviet Union support North Vietnam? (Asking Questions)

Extension Activity

Interview someone in your life who was alive during the Vietnam War. How did they learn about the war? Were they part of the military? Did they support or oppose the war? How do they feel now? Write a short report about the person's experience of the Vietnam War.

TABLE OF CONTENTS

KEY EVENTS

April 26, 1954:	The Geneva Conference begins, which will split . Vietnam into two countries
November 22, 1963:	President John F. Kennedy is assassinated
July 2, 1964:	President Lyndon B. Johnson signs the Civil Rights Act
August 10, 1964:	The Gulf of Tonkin Resolution comes into effect
January 31, 1968:	North Vietnamese and guerilla forces launch the . Tet Offensive
June 5, 1968:	Bobby Kennedy, candidate for president, is assassinated
July 20, 1969:	Neil Armstrong walks on the moon
December 1, 1969:	The draft lottery begins
May 4, 1970:	Four college students die in the Kent State shootings
January 27, 1973:	The Paris Peace Accords are signed, spelling out the end of the Vietnam War
August 9, 1974:	President Richard Nixon resigns
April 30, 1975:	Saigon, the capital of South Vietnam, falls to North Vietnam
November 13, 1982:	The Vietnam Veterans Memorial is dedicated in Washington, D.C.

CHAPTER ONE

THE COLD WAR IN ASIA

After the end of World War II in 1945, fear of communism gripped America. Although an **ally** of America during the war, the Soviet Union was under communist rule. Americans feared communism would spread around the world. The conflict with the United States and its allies against the Soviets and their allies became known as the Cold War.

This statue pays homage to Vladimir Lenin, founder of the Russian Communist Party and Soviet leader.

WHAT IS COMMUNISM?

Communism is a social, economic, and political system. In pure communism, people own all property together and are equal. But most people living in communist states have little freedom. They are unable to speak or practice religion freely. Communists wanted to spread their ideology all over the world. And for a time, it looked like they might be successful. Now, only five countries in the world are under communist rule: China, Cuba, Laos, Vietnam and North Korea.

The American public was terrified of nuclear war because both the U.S. and the Soviet Union had enough weapons to destroy each other. Leaders in both countries pulled back from a direct fight. Instead, most of the fighting of the Cold War would happen in weaker countries, such as Vietnam.

To prepare for nuclear war, students practiced ducking under desks. Families built fallout shelter designed to survive the deadly material that falls after a blast.

In 1954, Switzerland hosted Cold War rivals at the Geneva Conference. The conference split Vietnam in half. America supported South Vietnam. The Soviet Union and China backed North Vietnam, which wanted to reunite the country under communism. The North Vietnamese supported **guerrillas** fighting in South Vietnam.

The Indochina Wars were conflicts in Vietnam, Laos, and Cambodia, mainly involving France and later the United States. The wars are referred to as the French Indochina War and the Vietnam War.

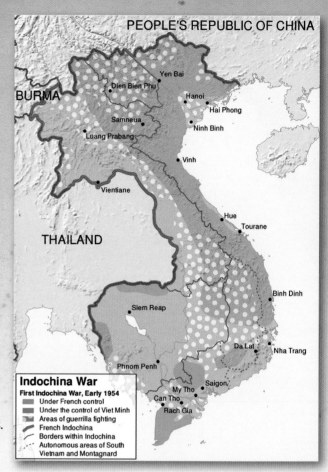

Indochina War
First Indochina War, Early 1954
- Under French control
- Under the control of Viet Minh
- Areas of guerrilla fighting
- French Indochina
- Borders within Indochina
- Autonomous areas of South Vietnam and Montagnard

President John F. Kennedy
1917 – 1963

Although most Americans knew very little about southeast Asia, opposing communism was very popular. America sent U.S. troops as advisors to South Vietnam along with military and economic aid. When Democrat John F. Kennedy became the U.S. president in 1961, he increased the soldiers and aid being sent.

FIGHTING THROUGH PEACE

*America and the Soviet Union fought for the favor of other nations. The Soviet Union sent some of its own citizens to help other communist countries. On March 1, 1961, Kennedy created the Peace Corps. The Peace Corps sent American **volunteers** to help communities around the world.*

Some soldiers were volunteers, but many were not. Although not officially at war, America had a **draft**, which called up an average of more than 120,000 young men a year between 1954 and 1964.

Many soldiers were minorities. Many were poor or working class. White men from wealthy families could often find ways to avoid military service.

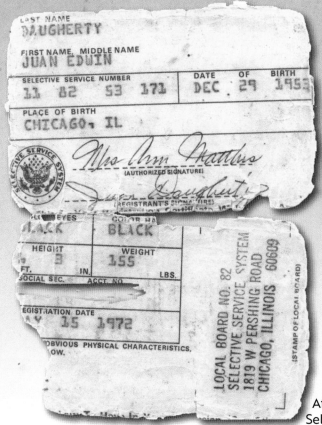

After registering with Selective Service, men received a card as proof. The law required men to keep these draft cards on them at all times.

TO SERVE, OR NOT TO SERVE

Local draft boards decided the fate of men ages 18 to 25. Men might avoid the draft by being in college, having a family, or by having an important job. A man could also avoid fighting by joining the National Guard, which was never sent to Vietnam.

CHAPTER TWO

THE WAR HEATS UP

President John F. Kennedy wondered whether America should stay in Vietnam or withdraw its forces. Before he could decide, tragedy struck. Kennedy was **assassinated** in Dallas, Texas, on November 22, 1963. While the country mourned, Vice President Lyndon B. Johnson was sworn in as the new president.

Johnson took the oath of office on Air Force One on the afternoon of Kennedy's death.

A PUBLIC FUNERAL

Many Americans loved the young and popular President Kennedy. Crowds lined the streets of Washington, D.C., to pay their respects as six horses pulled his casket past. Millions watched his funeral on television. Kennedy's widow had his funeral modeled on that of Abraham Lincoln, another assassinated president.

Johnson continued sending Americans to Vietnam. At the same time, Johnson created programs at home aimed at lifting Americans out of poverty and improving the conditions of people of color. He passed the Civil Rights Act of 1964, requiring people to be treated equally no matter their race or gender.

On July 2, 1964, politicians and civil rights leaders. including Martin Luther King Jr., looked on as Johnson signed the Civil Rights Act.

The economy was doing well. While the public worried as news of American deaths returned from Vietnam, they also worried about communism. As the 1964 election approached, Johnson's rival accused him of being too soft on the enemy.

Johnson's rival in 1964 was Arizona Senator Barry Goldwater, an opponent of the Civil Rights Act.

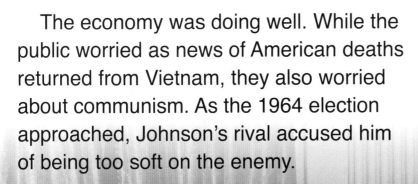

JOHNSON'S GREAT SOCIETY

Johnson had a vision for a "Great Society," and he tried to make his vision reality with new laws and new programs. The Wilderness Protection Act protected huge areas of land. Some new programs created jobs. Head Start prepared young children for school. Medicare provided health care for older Americans.

Reports arrived of a North Vietnamese attack on U.S. ships in the Gulf of Tonkin. The American public felt under attack. According to the U.S. Constitution, the president needed Congress to declare a war. On August 7, 1964, Congress passed the Gulf of Tonkin Resolution. It gave Johnson the power to wage war without a declaration of war.

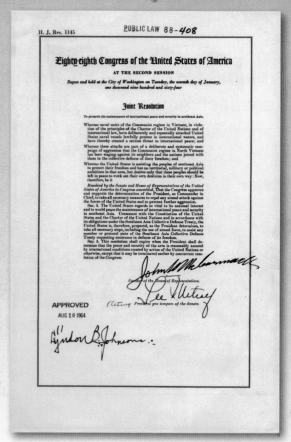

With the Gulf of Tonkin Resolution giving Johnson free rein, America's role in the conflict would expand dramatically.

THE GULF OF TONKIN INCIDENT

On August 2, 1964, a U.S. destroyer sailing the Gulf of Tonkin battled with North Vietnamese ships. During bad weather two days later, sailors on the destroyer thought they were being attacked again. They later realized they were mistaken. But Johnson and others misled the public by announcing two attacks.

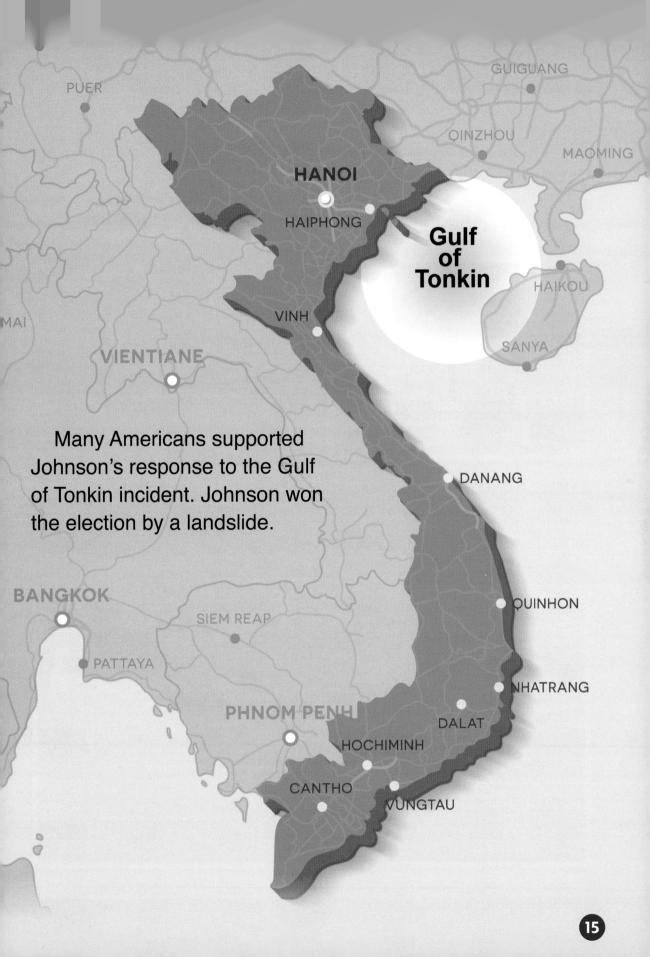

GUIGUANG

PUER

QINZHOU

MAOMING

HANOI

HAIPHONG

**Gulf
of
Tonkin**

HAIKOU

VINH

SANYA

VIENTIANE

MAI

Many Americans supported
Johnson's response to the Gulf
of Tonkin incident. Johnson won
the election by a landslide.

DANANG

BANGKOK

SIEM REAP

QUINHON

PATTAYA

NHATRANG

PHNOM PENH

DALAT

HOCHIMINH

CANTHO

VUNGTAU

CHAPTER THREE

WAR IN THE LIVING ROOM

In the spring of 1965, Johnson approved Operation Rolling Thunder, a campaign to bomb North Vietnam. The cost of fighting and number of Americans sent over soared. The draft increased to over 230,000 young men that year. Johnson looked for allies among other countries, but only five would eventually send troops.

Johnson hoped that Operation Rolling Thunder would convince the North Vietnamese to abandon the fight.

In addition to soldiers, hundreds of **journalists** from many nations headed to the battlefields of Vietnam. Americans at home had a front row seat to the conflict by watching television, listening to the radio, and reading the newspaper. Many journalists supported the war, but not all.

NEWS IN WAR

During the American Revolution, one-page newspapers spread the news. In the American Civil War, the public also followed the conflict through newspapers, which started including pictures. During World War II, the public saw war news at movie theaters. By Vietnam, many families had televisions in their living rooms.

Still, most Americans believed in the cause. But others were tired of seeing burning villages in Vietnam, or dead Americans brought home in body bags. Some thought America supported the wrong side. Some South Vietnamese leaders were dishonest, and many Vietnamese people supported the North.

Starting in 1965, professors and students held teach-ins at colleges to educate people about what their country was doing in Vietnam. In 1966, Americans were glued to their televisions as the Senate held hearings on the war. They learned the war was not going as well as they had thought.

The Beatles, who came to America from England, were among the many popular musicians who opposed the war.

YOUTHS RISE UP

Students were divided about Vietnam. A student group called Young Americans for Freedom supported the war. Students for a Democratic Society opposed it. Many young people became hippies, people who rejected the beliefs and behaviors of American society. Hippies wanted to spread love, not war.

In April of 1967, Martin Luther King Jr., an African-American hero of the civil rights movement, condemned the war in a fiery speech. He helped lead hundreds of thousands of protesters on a march to the United Nations building in New York City.

At the New York City march, King called for the United Nations to put pressure on America to end the bombing of North Vietnam.

Martin Luther King Jr.
1929 - 1968

MARTIN LUTHER KING JR.

Born in 1929, Martin Luther King Jr. became a civil rights leader in 1955 when he helped end segregation on public buses in Montgomery, Alabama. King rejected violence and preached equality. He spoke and led protests all over the country. At age 35 he received the Nobel Peace Prize.

CHAPTER FOUR

A CHANGE OF LEADERSHIP

As the presidential election of 1968 approached, the war was still going strong. However, only 32 percent of the American public approved of how Johnson was handling the war.

THE TET OFFENSIVE

January 31, 1968, was Tet, the Vietnamese New Year. During the holiday, North Vietnam forces and South Vietnamese guerrillas started a massive attack. Journalists recorded the desperate struggle, which left 1,100 Americans dead. American and South Vietnamese forces won the battle. But the public worried the war would never end.

After years of rising stock prices, the stock market would stutter as business growth slowed.

A high demand for goods and a weak dollar led to rising prices at stores.

The public was also unhappy about the economy. Vietnam and other costly American actions around the world were causing financial problems. Many Americans were out of work while prices had risen for goods and services.

Walter Cronkite was a news anchor who was trusted and well-liked by the public. At first, Cronkite supported the Vietnam War. When he visited Vietnam after the Tet Offensive, he grew convinced America would never win the war, even if they never lost. His announcement of this opinion became famous.

Johnson took to television to address the country directly. He called for peace talks, which might end the Vietnam War. At the same time, he announced he would not run for president again. His words shocked his listeners.

If not for the Vietnam War, Johnson might have run for election a second time.

Democratic candidate Bobby Kennedy, left, challenged Johnson's handling of the Vietnam War.

Republican candidate Richard Nixon vowed to end the war.

The public wanted to elect a president who would fix the country's problems. Many candidates fought to be their parties' nominee. The election campaigns brought up a lot of anger. One candidate, President Kennedy's brother Bobby Kennedy, was assassinated.

After Martin Luther King Jr.'s murder, riots broke out in more than 100 cities.

On April 4, 1968, Martin Luther King Jr. was also assassinated. African Americans and white Americans clashed in parts of the country. Protesters against the Vietnam War battled with police

Martin Luther King Jr. Memorial

outside the Democratic National Convention. Watching the news, it looked like the country was going up in flames.

In the summer of 1969, about 400,000 young people gathered in the rain and mud for the mythic Woodstock Music and Art Fair at a farm in Bethel, NY.

NIXON'S
THE ONE!

The Republican candidate, Richard Nixon, promised a return to law and order, including an end to the Vietnam War with honor. Nixon won the election.

THE SPACE RACE

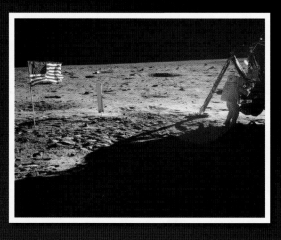

The Cold War spread beyond the atmosphere as America and the Soviets competed in space. In 1957, the Soviets put the first man-made object into orbit. In 1961, a Soviet man orbited Earth. But Americans reached the moon first, and Neil Armstrong walked on its surface on July 20, 1969.

CHAPTER FIVE

COUNTER-EVERYTHING

Once Nixon became president, he pushed a plan for South Vietnamese troops to take over the fighting. But American troop numbers remained high. The government tried to make the draft fairer by using a **lottery** system, starting on December 1, 1969.

It was illegal to burn draft cards, but doing so became a popular activity at protests.

Folk singer Phil Ochs composed antiwar songs and sang at political events.

More young men faced the possibility of being sent to fight a war in Southeast Asia. Feelings against the war spread. Some young men burned their draft cards to show their opposition. Huge protests took to the streets.

RESISTING THE DRAFT

Men who opposed the conflict, or who feared facing the horrors of war, tried to escape the draft in different ways. Hundreds of thousands never reported when called up. Some fled to Canada. Some men pretended to have health problems or claimed a religious objection to fighting.

Heavyweight boxing champion Muhammad Ali publicly resisted the draft.

Some people accused the protesters of supporting communism. Nixon turned to what he called the "Silent Majority," the Americans who still approved of the Vietnam War. Some working-class people, struggling to make ends meet and annoyed by the protests, took to the streets themselves.

In 1969, a group of American Indians took over Alcatraz Island in San Francisco Bay to protest government actions toward native groups.

Along with protests about the war, many other movements rocked the country. Minorities, including African Americans and American Indians, continued to fight for civil rights. Some women banded together to push for equal treatment compared to men. Gay people joined together to fight for equality and civil rights. The environmental movement began.

About 20 million Americans celebrated the first Earth Day, drawing attention to environmental issues.

The Kent State Shootings drew the sympathy of the American public toward the protesters.

COLLEGE SHOOTINGS

In May of 1970, the National Guard was called in to Kent State University in Ohio. During a heated clash with protesters on May 4, guardsmen shot and killed four unarmed students. The deaths rocked the country. Eleven days later, police killed two students at Jackson State University in Mississippi.

Nixon hoped to shorten the war, and strengthen public support, by attacking North Vietnamese positions in neighboring countries.

The media brought news of protests around the world, some against the Vietnam War. Americans worried about their reputation abroad. Many people around the world condemned American actions in the war. Even as the number of U.S. troops finally dropped, U.S. bombing spread from Vietnam to neighboring Cambodia and Laos.

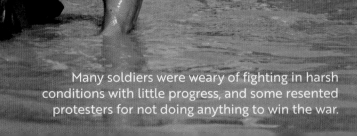

Many soldiers were weary of fighting in harsh conditions with little progress, and some resented protesters for not doing anything to win the war.

CHEMICALS OF WAR

People objected to napalm and Agent Orange, two chemicals used by the U.S. military in Vietnam. Napalm is a sticky substance which burns long and hot. Agent Orange kills plants. The military used it to destroy jungles in which guerrillas hid. Agent Orange caused health problems

PULLING OUT OF VIETNAM

In 1971, parts of the **Pentagon** Papers, a report on America's history in Vietnam, was leaked to journalists. The report had been meant for the government's eyes only, not for the public. Newspapers started publishing the papers. Nixon's **administration** tried to stop them, but failed.

At first, Nixon, left, wondered if the Pentagon Papers might even help his standing with the public, since the papers covered events before his presidency.

The public began to glimpse the full story of their country's actions in the war. Presidents and their administrations had been misleading the public about the Vietnam War for years. Unlike at the beginning of the war, now the public was less scared of communism and was sick of American soldiers dying.

NIXON VISITS CHINA

In 1972, Nixon became the first U.S. president in 22 years to travel to the People's Republic of China while in office. He met with Chairman Mao Zedong and the Chinese Premier, Zhou Enlai. The week-long visit didn't solve all conflicts between the two countries, but it improved their relations.

Public opinion of American troops was suffering. Reports spread of soldiers deserting or disobeying orders. The public heard stories of U.S. soldiers killing civilians, or even their own officers. The Vietnam War continued to hurt America's standing around the world.

In 1971, Lieutenant William Calley was convicted of murder for ordering U.S. soldiers to shoot hundreds of Vietnamese civilians in the village of My Lai.

Nixon began reaching out to America's Cold War rivals. He also began to end the war. Troop levels finally dropped, although bombings increased. On January 27, 1973, the U.S. and North Vietnam signed the Paris Peace Accords, which created a road map for a ceasefire.

Nixon called the Senate Watergate hearings a witch hunt, but the evidence continued to mount against him.

A PRESIDENT BEHAVING BADLY

In 1972, police arrested five men at the Watergate offices in Washington, D.C. The men had broken into the headquarters of the Democratic Party. The break-in was linked to the Nixon campaign, which wanted to spy on rivals. Nixon tried to cover up this and other misconduct, but failed.

Taking over from Nixon, President Gerald Ford would oversee the bitter end of the Vietnam War.

Nixon's accomplishments in foreign and national politics were overshadowed by the end of his time in the White House.

The end came too late for Nixon. His dishonest actions against his political rivals were slowly coming to light. The discoveries would lead the disgraced president to resign on August 9, 1974.

Congress passed the War Powers Act, which checked the power of presidents to wage war without approval. U.S. soldiers soon headed home. A small number stayed as advisors until North Vietnam conquered the south in 1975.

Almost two million refugees left Vietnam after the war.

GETTING OUT OF SAIGON

In April of 1975, Americans left Saigon, the capital of South Vietnam. Over 19 hours, the U.S. military flew out more than 1,000 Americans and 5,000 South Vietnamese. Tens of thousands more South Vietnamese fled the country by air or sea. On April 30, North Vietnamese soldiers took the city.

CHAPTER SEVEN

AFTER VIETNAM

The U.S. Congress never officially declared war in Vietnam. Yet over 58,000 Americans had died. Vietnam was hammered, with as many as 3 million civilians and fighters dead. The conflict cost America over 170 billion dollars. The U.S. economy had been booming at the beginning of the war, but now it struggled.

Built in 1982, the Vietnam Veterans Memorial honored all the **veterans** who died in the conflict.

Hundreds of thousands of veterans returned home to find that jobs were scarce. Over 153,000 soldiers had been wounded. Some were tormented by what they had seen and done during the war.

Arizona Senator John McCain returned home a hero after North Vietnam shot down his plane and kept him in prison for five years.

VETERANS AFTER THE WAR

Many Vietnam veterans had trouble adapting to life in America again, but many succeeded. Arizona Senator John McCain and director Oliver Stone are two of the many famous people who fought in the war. Years later, thousands of veterans have visited Vietnam to help make sense of their experiences.

Some veterans wondered why they had been fighting, while others wondered why the American public hadn't supported them. In return, many civilians who felt uncomfortable about the war didn't know how to treat the returning veterans, or even acted angrily towards them.

The Vietnam Veterans Memorial includes the Three Soldiers, right, a tribute to the diverse people who fought the war. Nearby on the the National Mall is the Korean War Veterans Memorial, below, which honors veterans from the less controversial conflict running from 1950 to 1953.

The U.S. draft is gone—for now. Congress and the president could restart it using the Selective Service. Male citizens ages 18 to 25 still register for Selective Service, as well as men from other countries who've moved to America. Men who don't register lose out on federal benefits.

The draft had ended. After the Vietnam War, the U.S. military would consist of all volunteers. However, young people from wealthy families were still less likely to volunteer for military service.

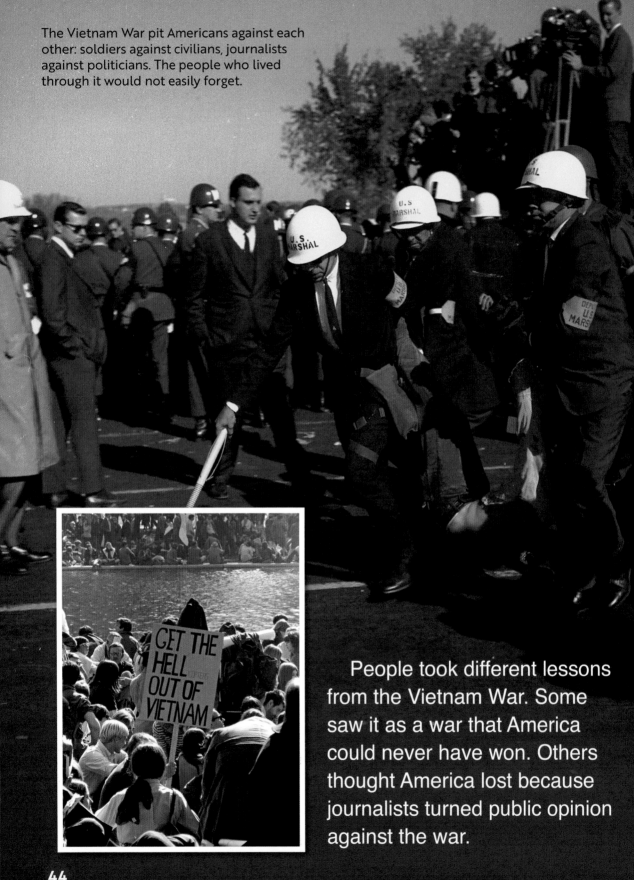

The Vietnam War pit Americans against each other: soldiers against civilians, journalists against politicians. The people who lived through it would not easily forget.

People took different lessons from the Vietnam War. Some saw it as a war that America could never have won. Others thought America lost because journalists turned public opinion against the war.

In future wars, the military would tightly control journalists. It would also hesitate to send in ground troops, because the public had reacted poorly to the deaths of American soldiers. For many Americans, their trust in their own government and military had been greatly shaken.

A CHANGE IN REPORTING

As many as 600 journalists from different countries covered the Vietnam War at one time. Although many reporters stayed in the capital, Saigon, others roamed freely. More than 60 died. In the 1991 Gulf War, the U.S. military controlled the movements of U.S. journalists and reviewed their stories before publication.

GLOSSARY

administration (ad-min-i-STRAY-shuhn): a president's government, including cabinet leaders and advisors

ally (AL-eye): one country which supports another, especially during war

assassinated (uh-SAS-uh-nay-tid): murdered for political reasons

draft (draft): a system for choosing people who must join the military

guerrillas (guh-RIL-uhs): small groups of fighters who are not part of an official army

journalists (JUR-nuh-lists): people who report on the news

lottery (LAH-tur-ee): a drawing to choose something or someone

Pentagon (PEN-tuh-gahn): the headquarters of the U.S. military in Washington, D.C.

veterans (VET-ur-uhns): people who have been soldiers

volunteers (vah-luhn-TEERS): people who offer to do a job

INDEX

SHOW WHAT YOU KNOW

1. Why did many Americans support the Vietnam War?
2. What was one thing that turned Americans against the war?
3. What was a movement in America during the Vietnam War other than the one against the war itself?
4. How did Nixon end the Vietnam War?
5. What did the War Powers Act do?

FURTHER READING

Burgan, Michael, *Death at Kent State: How a Photograph Brought the Vietnam War Home to America*, Compass Point Books, 2017.

Otfinoski, Steven, *The Vietnam War (A Step into History)*, Children's Press, 2017.

Sherman, Jill, *The Vietnam War: 12 Things to Know*, 12-Story Library, 2017.

ABOUT THE AUTHOR

Clara MacCarald is a children's book author with a master's degree in biology. She lives with her family in an off-grid house nestled in the forests of central New York. When not parenting her daughter, she spends her time writing nonfiction books for kids.

www.rourkeeducationalmedia.com

Photo Credits: Cover: map © Uwe Dedering https://creativecommons.org/licenses/by-sa/3.0/deed.en cover photos courtesy of U.S. Military; other photos istock.com, shutterstock.com except: PG4; wjarosz, lukbar. PG5; U.S. National Archives. Pg5; Courtesy Library of Congress. Pg6; Dzyuba, Pg7;Snyde88, USPC. Pg8; Courtesy- USmil. Pg9; Courtesy Library of Congresy. Pg10; Courtesy Library of Congress. Pg11; Courtesy Library of Congress. Pg13; Courtesy Library of Congress Pg14;Snyde88, USAF. Pg15; USAF. Pg16; USAF. Pg17; Courtesy Library of Congress, Courtesy National Archives. Pg18; mil.gov. Pg19;effler, Warren K. Author; Leena A. Krohn (CCA-Share Alike 3.0), Eric Koch, Nationaal Archief, Den Haag, Rijksfotoarchief: Fotocollectie Algemeen Nederlands Fotopersbureau (ANEFO)—www.gahetna.nl. PG20;mizoula. Pg21; World Telegram & Sun photo by Dick DeMarsico. Pg22;USAF Pg23: North Carolina State Archives, Raleigh, NC. Pg24; Public Domain. Pg25; Leffler, Warren K., photographer, Gift: Gary Yanker; 1975-1983. Pg26; Laura Choate via (CCA-ShareAlike 3.0), LOC- U.S. News & World Report. Pg27; ift; Gary Yanker; 1975-1983, Mark Goff, NASA Pg28; Jack E. Kightlinger (White House Photo Office), by Marion S. Trisoko & Thomas J. O'Halloran, Phil Ochs outside the offices of the National Student Association in Washington, DC. 1975 Source;Own work-CC BY-SA 3.0. January 1965, uwdigitalcollections -Creative Commons Attribution 2.0 General. Pg29; LofC-Ira Rosenberg, Leffler, Warren K. Pg30; George Garrigues, Tewy-GNU-CCA-Share Alike 3.0, Pg31; Street Protest TV (CCA 2.0 Generic). Pg32; Sam Stadener, usa mil.gov. Pg33; Us.mil, US Army. Pg34; Nixon Library/National Archives, Nixon Library Pg35;Courtesy Library of Congress, Courtesy National Archives. PG36; mil.gov. Pg37; Knudsen, Robert L. Pg38; shutterstock.com. Pg39: Gerald R. Ford Presidential Library and Museum. Pg40; mil.gov. PG41; US.DOD, SeanPavonePhoto. Pg42; Pierdelune, RomanBabakin. Pg43; mil.gov Pg44; Courtesy Library of Congress. Pg45; Nick Ut

Edited by: Keli Sipperley

Produced by Blue Door Education for Rourke Educational Media. Cover and Interior design by: Jennifer Dydyk

Living Through the Vietnam War / Clara MacCarald
(American Culture and Conflict)
ISBN 978-1-64156-418-2 (hard cover)
ISBN 978-1-64156-544-8 (soft cover)
ISBN 978-1-64156-667-4 (e-Book)
Library of Congress Control Number: 2018930438

Rourke Educational Media

Printed in the United States of America, North Mankato, Minnesota